W9-CIN-213

DISNEY's
THE HUNCHBACK
OF NOTRE DAME

High up in the bell tower of the Cathedral of Notre Dame lived the bell ringer known as Quasimodo. Born with a misshapen body, but a gentle soul, Quasimodo was forbidden by his master, Judge Claude Frollo, from ever leaving his lonely home.

Quasimodo had some unusual companions in the bell tower. They were three of the cathedral's stone gargoyles, who came to life only for him. Together, they looked down on the streets of Paris, watching the rest of the world pass Quasimodo by.

Quasimodo's favorite time for watching the crowds was the Festival of Fools. All of Paris took to the streets in celebration, putting on masks, and crowning the person with the ugliest mask as the King of Fools. How he longed to join in!

This year, encouraged by his gargoyle friends, Quasimodo decided to go to the festival and join the fun—even though Frollo had forbidden it.

Out in the square, another young man was making his way through the crowd. His name was Phoebus, and he had just returned to Paris to work as Frollo's Captain of the Guard.

Unsure where to go, he stopped to ask for directions. It was then that he spied Esmeralda, the most beautiful woman he'd ever seen. But before he could say a word, two soldiers accused the gypsy woman of stealing and tried to drag her away. Phoebus blocked the soldiers' way with his horse, and Esmeralda and her goat ran off to the festival.

Meanwhile, Quasimodo found his way to the crowded festival convinced that he would not be noticed. To his surprise, he was noticed. Standing in a line of contestants all wearing masks, Quasimodo was crowned the King of Fools by Clopin, the gypsy leader.

"Here he is—Quasimodo, the Hunchback of Notre Dame," yelled Clopin. And with that, the crowd picked the bell ringer up, put him on their shoulders, and paraded him through the streets of Paris.

Quasimodo's joy at finally fitting in was too much for Frollo's soldiers. They began to tease him and throw food at him.

Soon everyone joined in. Tied up and frightened, he begged his master Frollo to help him. But Frollo refused. He wanted to teach Quasimodo a lesson.

This was more than the kindhearted Esmeralda could bear. She came forward to defend Quasimodo.

Furious, Frollo ordered Esmeralda's capture, but she escaped unharmed. Disguising herself as a beggar, the gypsy hid in Notre Dame. Frollo found her but could not arrest her; he was powerless inside the cathedral.

One soft-spoken voice came to her rescue as she climbed up to the bell tower. "You helped me," Quasimodo offered. "Now I will help you."

Quasimodo carried Esmeralda down the side of the bell tower to freedom. In gratitude, she took off the necklace she always wore and gave it to him. The necklace with its secret meaning would be a way Quasimodo could find her if he ever needed help.

No sooner had Esmeralda disappeared when Phoebus came to the cathedral looking for her. Believing that Phoebus meant to harm Esmeralda, Quasimodo insisted that he leave.

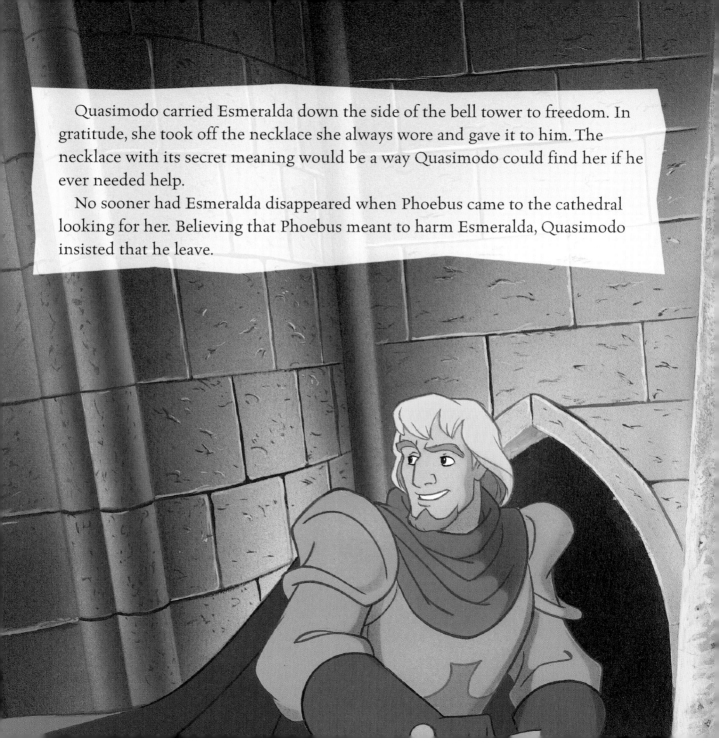

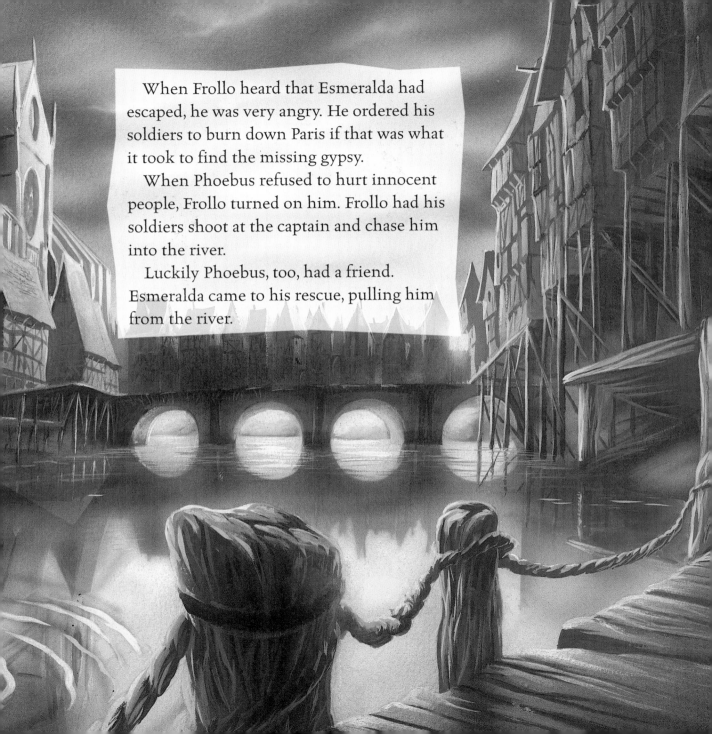

When Frollo heard that Esmeralda had escaped, he was very angry. He ordered his soldiers to burn down Paris if that was what it took to find the missing gypsy.

When Phoebus refused to hurt innocent people, Frollo turned on him. Frollo had his soldiers shoot at the captain and chase him into the river.

Luckily Phoebus, too, had a friend. Esmeralda came to his rescue, pulling him from the river.

After taking the wounded Phoebus to Quasimodo for safekeeping, Esmeralda fled to the Court of Miracles, the gypsies' hiding place. Phoebus and Quasimodo soon followed after learning of Frollo's plans for the gypsies.

But Frollo surprised them all at the Court of Miracles. Taking Phoebus and all the gypsies as prisoners, he turned to Quasimodo. "Take him back to the bell tower, and make sure he stays there!" Frollo told his men. They followed his orders by chaining Quasimodo to pillars high in the cathedral.

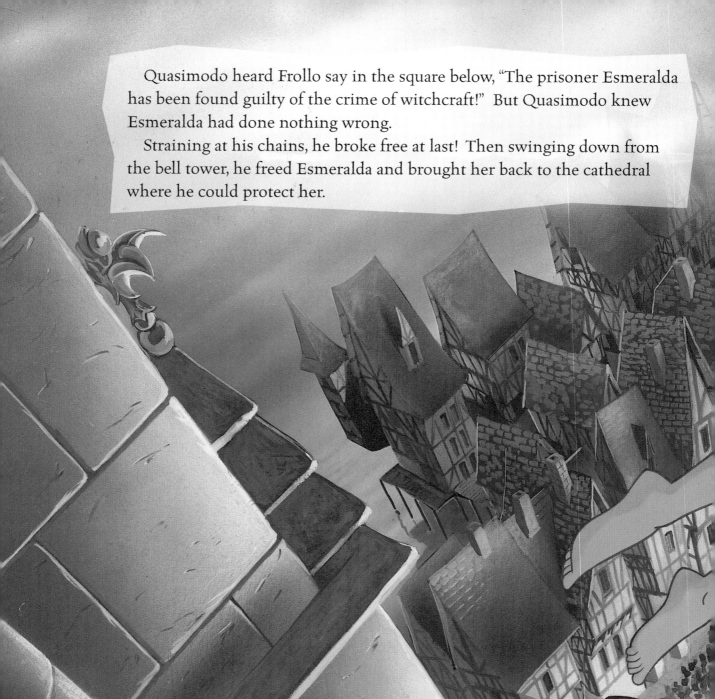

Quasimodo heard Frollo say in the square below, "The prisoner Esmeralda has been found guilty of the crime of witchcraft!" But Quasimodo knew Esmeralda had done nothing wrong.

Straining at his chains, he broke free at last! Then swinging down from the bell tower, he freed Esmeralda and brought her back to the cathedral where he could protect her.

Frollo ordered his soldiers to attack Notre Dame. With determination, Quasimodo found the strength of ten men that day. Joined by the gargoyles, Phoebus, and the gypsies, he eventually defeated the soldiers.

But Frollo refused to give up. He slipped inside the church, and searched for the helpless Esmeralda, wanting to harm her and Quasimodo.

As Frollo reached out to strike Esmeralda and Quasimodo, he fell to the street below. The people rejoiced to see goodness win over evil. They raised the bell ringer of Notre Dame to their shoulders once more. Quasimodo was no longer the King of Fools, but a hero for all time.